- **Book Name**

- Technology in Education

- **Written by**

- Sam Berman

• Title

- "From Pixels to Progress: How Technology is Reshaping the Educational Landscape"

Table of Contents

Chapter 1.The Revolution in Online Education

- What we call "The Digital Classroom Revolution" is really just a paradigm shift in education that has occurred as a result of using digital tools in more conventional settings. This shift away from traditional methods of instruction is characterized by the adoption of cutting-edge resources with the goal of improving education for all parties involved.

-
  The Digital Classroom Revolution's essential components are:
- Interactive whiteboards, tablets, and instructional software and applications are just a few examples of the technology tools that are finding their way into conventional classrooms. The goal of this integration is to make the learning environment more engaging and participatory.
- Students are able to actively participate in their own education through the use of digital classrooms, which promote interactive learning. Various learning styles can be accommodated through the use of interactive multimedia, simulations, and digital resources, which allow for a more hands-on approach to learning.
- Students now have instantaneous access to a treasure trove of information online, thanks to the digital revolution in the classroom. Their

ability to delve deeply into subjects, perform research, and keep up with current events is enhanced by this access, which promotes a mindset of lifelong learning.

- Tools for Collaboration: Students and teachers are able to work together more easily with the help of technology. By eliminating physical distance and facilitating real-time communication and group projects, digital tools like virtual classes and collaborative documents encourage cooperation and overcome geographical obstacles.

- Individualized Instruction: With the help of digital resources, teachers can create lessons just for their students. Online evaluations, educational apps, and adaptive learning tools allow teachers to meet the needs of students with varying learning styles and speeds.

- The opportunities for remote learning have been greatly enhanced by the digital revolution, which has sped up the acceptance of this method and given both students and teachers more freedom. With the advent of virtual classrooms and other online collaboration technologies, education is no longer limited to the four walls of a conventional school.

- Technology has made it possible to gather and analyze data on student engagement and performance, leading to data-driven education. Teachers can utilize this data to hone in on

student strengths, pinpoint problem areas, and tailor their support accordingly.

- The goal of the digital classroom revolution is to prepare students for the modern world by teaching them how to effectively use digital tools. In an academic and professional world where digital fluency is becoming more important, students who are exposed to a variety of technologies are better prepared for the future.

- As a whole, the advent of the digital classroom has marked a sea change in the way schools operate, with an emphasis on making use of students' unique interests and needs to design lessons that are more interactive, relevant, and successful.

Chapter 2.Virtual and augmented reality as tools for immersive learning experiences

- The term "Immersive Learning Experiences: Virtual and Augmented Reality in Education" describes the use of AR and VR to improve and revolutionize conventional classrooms. These innovations in technology are reshaping the way we educate by immersing students in dynamic and engaging experiences.

-
  Important features of VR/AR-based immersive learning experiences are as follows:
- Augmented reality (AR):
- Visualization and Simulation: Virtual reality (VR) transports users to digital recreations of real-world locations, allowing them to experience firsthand things like virtual field trips, historical sites, or scientific experiments. If you're looking for an alternative to boring old textbooks or boring old lectures, this will provide you with a much better education. Interactive Learning: Virtual reality makes it possible to learn by doing in environments that would be too dangerous or impracticable to do in the actual world. Students of medicine, for instance, can hone their surgical abilities in a simulated setting before stepping foot in a real

operating   room.

What is augmented reality (AR)?

- Augmented reality (AR) superimposes digital information on top of the physical world. One application in education is the enhancement of traditional learning materials with the addition of 3D models, animations, or more information when a device is pointed at a textbook. Augmented reality (AR) improves visualization by superimposing digital data onto real-world objects. This can be useful in anatomy classes, as students can view digital organs superimposed on real-life models.

Personal Involvement and Communication:

- Engaged Learning: Instead of just watching, students in immersive learning environments are encouraged to actively participate. Students can gain a deeper knowledge of the material through more interactive and hands-on engagement with things, environments, and content. Immersion: Students are captivated by VR and AR, which enhances their learning experience and makes it more pleasurable. A more positive outlook on learning and better information retention are common outcomes of this kind of enhanced involvement.

Tailored Instruction:

- Personalization: Virtual reality and augmented reality can be adjusted to fit the preferences and learning styles of each user. An adaptive and personalized learning experience is fostered when students may go at their own pace, concentrate on what interests them, and get feedback tailored to their specific needs. Worldwide Educational Possibilities:

- Collaborating Virtually: Virtual reality enables students from diverse regions of the globe to work together in shared virtual environments, cultivating cross-cultural understanding and global relationships. Students can learn about historical landmarks, natural wonders, and scientific phenomena without ever having to leave their seats, thanks to augmented reality technology that can transport them to faraway places. Use in the Actual World:

- Preparedness for the Workforce: By modeling real-world work situations, immersive learning experiences get students ready for the workforce. Industries, including healthcare, engineering, and aviation, stand to gain the most from this. The use of VR and AR in the classroom changes the way students learn by giving them more agency over their own learning and providing them with novel tools to investigate, comprehend, and engage with course material.

Chapter 3: AI for Education: Customizing the Educational Experience

- With an emphasis on adapting educational experiences to each student's unique requirements, "Artificial Intelligence in Education: Personalizing the Learning Journey" delves into the revolutionary effects of AI on the educational sector as a whole. The goal of incorporating AI into classrooms is to make learning more dynamic, responsive, and tailored to each student.
- The important parts of AI in the classroom and how it helps students study at their own pace are as follows:
- Personalized Educational Routes:
- Adaptive learning pathways are generated by AI algorithms that examine data on individual students' performance, preferences, and learning styles. This way, students may go through the lessons at their own speed while still getting the individualized attention they need to succeed. Content delivery with a personal twist:
- Personalized instructional content is curated and delivered by AI systems. Individualized instruction takes into account each student's strengths, weaknesses, learning style, and pace

through the use of interactive simulations and supplemental materials. Improved engagement and understanding are outcomes of personalized content distribution.

Immediate Criticism and Evaluation:

- With the help of AI, we can now evaluate student work in real-time and provide them with immediate comments. Students are able to quickly pinpoint their weak spots, clear up any misunderstandings, and reinforce their learning goals with the help of this feedback loop.

Analytics for the Future:

- To predict how well a student will do in the future using their past performance data, predictive analytics use artificial intelligence systems. If the system foresees difficulties, teachers can step in early and give extra help to keep students on course.

Adaptive Evaluation:

- AI-driven adaptive testing personalizes evaluations based on students' actual strengths and areas for improvement. In order to alleviate exam anxiety and provide a more accurate reflection of the student's knowledge, the questions' difficulty levels are adaptive.

Systems for Intelligent Tutoring:

- Virtual instructors powered by AI can provide one-on-one help and direction. To make sure that each student has a personalized learning experience, these systems modify their methods of instruction depending on what the students say.

Finding Recurring Patterns in Learning:

- AI systems can analyze student learning patterns, providing instructors with valuable insights on how diverse individuals tackle and excel in different subjects. Curriculum development and pedagogical practices can greatly benefit from this data.

Made More Accessible:

- Because they can adapt to different types of learning, AI systems can make education more accessible. Some examples of AI-powered features that help students with diverse learning skills are text-to-speech and speech-to-text.

Streamlined Company Procedures:

- AI simplifies administrative work, freeing up educators to devote more time to instruction. Personalized student contact can now take place thanks to the automation of grading, data analysis, and mundane administrative tasks.

Improving Over Time:

- Through interactions and feedback from users, AI systems are always learning and adapting. The customization of instructional content and delivery can be enhanced continuously through this iterative learning process. To sum up, the use of AI in the classroom signifies a major turn towards tailoring the educational experience to each individual student. Teachers can better meet their students' individual needs with the help of AI's data-driven insights and adaptable technology, creating an environment that is more welcoming, interesting, and productive for everyone.

Chapter 4. Gamification and Edutainment: A Game-Based Approach to Education

- Of course! We'll begin with "Artificial Intelligence in Education: Personalizing the Learning Journey."

- Utilizing AI in the Classroom: Crafting a Unique Educational Experience for Each Student
- The idea behind this is to use AI in teaching methods so that each student can have a unique and tailored educational experience. Some important points are:
- Personalized Educational Routes:
- In order to design personalized learning programs, AI systems examine each student's past work, current habits, and preferred methods of learning. This makes sure that every student gets personalized content, so they may learn at their own speed and concentrate on the areas where they're struggling. Efficient Distribution of Media:
- Depending on the interests and skill level of the student, AI can either suggest or create content. In order to improve comprehension and involvement, this involves proposing supplemental materials, interactive exercises, or

multimedia   resources.
Immediate Criticism:

- With the help of AI, students can get immediate comments on their work. Students are able to quickly recognize and fix their errors thanks to this feedback loop, which strengthens their learning and promotes a more thorough comprehension of the subject.
Systems for Intelligent Tutoring:

- AI-driven tutoring platforms cater to each student's unique requirements by tailoring their approach to instruction. The student's progress and obstacles can inform these systems' provision of more explanations, examples, or assignments.

Decisions Backed by Data:

- AI sifts through mountains of data on how well students do in class, how they act, and how they learn. These findings can help teachers make better decisions, pinpoint problem areas, and create individualized plans to help their pupils who are having difficulty learning.
Analytics for the Future:

- By analyzing past data, AI algorithms can foretell how a lesson will go. In this way, teachers may foresee problems before they happen and step in before they spiral out of control, giving them the best chance for success.
Made More Accessible:

- Students with various learning needs can benefit from AI's improved accessibility. Tools powered by artificial intelligence (AI), such as speech recognition and customizable interfaces, contribute to making the classroom more welcoming to all students. Efficient Evaluation and Grading:

- With the help of AI, teachers are free to concentrate on instruction and student-specific support rather than mundane grading duties. A more simplified learning experience may result from its effectiveness. The use of AI in the classroom allows for a more dynamic, individual, and productive educational experience. The educational experience as a whole becomes more engaging and fruitful, students receive individualized assistance, and teachers acquire insightful knowledge.
- Continuing, we have "Gamification and Edutainment: Learning Through Play."
- Engaging in Game-Based Learning: A New Approach to Edutainment
- This idea proposes enhancing engagement and motivation in educational activities by adding aspects of game design and entertainment. Some important points are:
- Interactive Features:
- The term "gamification" refers to the practice of incorporating gaming mechanics into non-game settings, most notably the use of points, levels, badges, and prizes. Students are motivated to continue through learning assignments and experience a sense of achievement because of

these aspects.
Narratives and Storytelling:

- Edutainment is the practice of presenting instructional knowledge through narratives and stories in an engaging and enjoyable manner. Students are more likely to remain interested and absorb information when educational objectives are woven into an engaging plot. Experiential Learning Through Interaction:

- The focus of gamification and education is on making learning more engaging and participatory. Active engagement is key in these types of learning environments, which might take the form of simulations, role-playing scenarios, or educational games. The Rivalry and the Cooperation:

- Gamification frequently incorporates elements of competition, allowing students to challenge themselves or their peers to reach higher scores or levels. Collaborative games also foster a sense of community among students by encouraging them to work together. Speedy Response:

- Learning through trial and error is reinforced by the rapid feedback that games provide on actions and decisions. Students are able to better grasp the outcomes of their actions and are motivated to improve their techniques through this immediate feedback loop. The Power of Internal Drive:

- Students are able to immerse themselves further in their learning journey when they utilize the intrinsic incentive found in games. A positive attitude toward learning is enhanced by the excitement and fulfillment that come from accomplishing tasks or finding solutions to issues. Use in the Actual World:

- One way that education helps students recognize the value of what they are studying is by relating theoretical ideas to practical situations. Making this real-world link can help with both comprehension and memorization. Adaptability and flexibility

- Learning can be made more flexible using gamification, which caters to a variety of learning styles and paces. A more individualized learning experience is fostered by allowing students to move through the content at their own pace. Teachers can make class more interesting and fun for students by using gamification and edutainment techniques; this will encourage them to participate more and develop a passion for studying.

Chapter 5: Educational Technology and Inclusive Education: Conquering Obstacles and Closing Gaps

- "EdTech and Inclusive Education: Bridging Gaps and Breaking Barriers" explores how educational technology (EdTech) has an enormous influence on promoting inclusive practices in schools. All students, regardless of their socioeconomic status, physical ability, or other personal factors, should be able to participate fully and successfully in the educational system, and this investigation centers on how technology can help to do just that.

-

  Important parts of this subject matter comprise:
- Learner-Friendly Materials:
- In order to meet the demands of students with a wide range of learning styles, EdTech solutions make a wide variety of learning materials easily available. Making education more accessible for students with various abilities is made possible by adaptable technologies, multimedia content, and configurable interfaces. Individualized Courses of Study:
- With the help of EdTech, individualized lesson plans can be developed for each student. In order to tailor their material and support to each

student's needs, adaptive learning platforms analyze data and algorithms to determine each student's strengths and areas for improvement. Various learning styles and speeds can be accommodated by this tailored method.
Adaptive Devices:

- Students with physical or mental impairments can benefit from EdTech solutions that use assistive technologies. Supporting a more inclusive learning environment for students with visual, auditory, or movement impairments is technology such as screen readers, text-to-speech tools, and speech recognition software. Distance Education Programs:

- By removing physical distance from the learning process, online learning environments and virtual classrooms help to promote inclusive education. Collaborative learning opportunities and high-quality education are accessible to students from all over the world, even those in underprivileged or rural places. Representation of Diverse Content:

- EdTech advocates for the inclusion of cultural content and varied viewpoints in educational resources. A sense of community and understanding of other cultures can flourish when kids from all walks of life can find a place in the classroom. Assistance with Languages:

- The provision of language-learning applications, translation tools, and other language support features is one way in which EdTech may help overcome language obstacles. Because of this, all students, regardless of their native language, will have equal access to course materials. Adaptable Methods of Instruction:

- With the help of EdTech, students with different schedules and preferences can have access to a variety of learning modes. Students with special requirements or limited access to time can still take advantage of asynchronous learning opportunities, such as recorded lectures and interactive modules. Practices for Inclusive Evaluation:

- With the help of technology, inclusive assessment procedures are becoming more feasible, and new kinds of evaluation are emerging. The use of assistive technology during tests, project-based assessments, or interactive assessments can all fall under this category, with the goal of shifting the focus from standard metrics to students' actual knowledge and skills. Teachers' Opportunities for Professional Growth:

- In order to help teachers become more proficient in inclusive teaching, EdTech offers continuous professional development opportunities. Teachers are able to better accommodate students from a variety of backgrounds by making good use of technology in the classroom, thanks to training programs and tools. This theme delves into the relationship between educational technology (EdTech) and inclusive education, shedding light on how technology may help remove obstacles, provide equal access to education, and cultivate a welcoming classroom for all students.

Chapter 6: The Expansion of E-Learning and Other Online Learning Platforms

- The article "The Rise of Online Learning Platforms: E-Learning and Beyond" delves into the revolutionary shift in education away from conventional classrooms and into the vast realm of online learning. This overarching theme highlights the influence and development of several e-learning platforms, highlighting the breadth of e-learning outside of traditional classrooms.

-

Important parts of this subject matter comprise:

- Convenience and adaptability:
- The convenience of online learning systems is second to none; students can access course materials from any location with an internet connection. Education becomes more accessible to individuals with various schedules, allowing them to balance work, family, and other commitments.

A Wide Range of Courses Offered:

- Courses on e-learning platforms include a broad range of topics and are suitable for students of all abilities. Without regard to physical location, students can participate in formal education, research areas of interest, or advance their careers.

Learning with Interactivity and Multimedia:

- Interactive features, multimedia resources, and interesting content elevate online education above that of static textbooks. The use of collaborative tools, video lectures, simulations, and quizzes improves the learning experience and accommodates various learning styles.

Independent Study:

- Students can go through the material at their own speed, which is a hallmark of online education. Students benefit from self-paced courses because they may go back over difficult material as many times as they need to, focus on subjects that really interest them, and tailor their learning experience to their specific requirements.

Communities of Global Learners:

- The development of inclusive and worldwide learning communities is facilitated by online learning platforms. Through a multicultural lens, students from all over the globe may work together, exchange ideas, and have meaningful conversations, enhancing the quality of their education.

Career Advancement and Skill Enhancement:

- In order to advance one's career and acquire new skills, online learning platforms are invaluable. Targeted courses are available to professionals so they may improve their abilities, keep up with their industries, and adjust to the changing demands of the work market. Technologies for Adaptive Learning:

- In order to make learning on some platforms more tailored to each individual, adaptive learning technologies are used. In order to maximize each student's comprehension and retention, these technologies analyze their unique strengths and weaknesses and modify the course material and learning pace accordingly. Engaging with Gamification:

- Incorporating gamification features like interactive challenges, badges, and awards into online learning platforms is a common way to boost participation. Learners are motivated by these factors, which enhance the educational process and promote persistent engagement. Opportunities for Lifelong Learning:

- By making it possible for people to keep studying even after they've left school, online education bolsters the idea of lifelong learning. Learners have the opportunity to expand their skill sets, indulge in personal interests, or delve into uncharted academic territory at any point in their lives.

The Rise of Massive Open Online Courses and MOOCs:

- One major component of the growth of online education is MOOCs, or Massive Open Online Courses. By making world-class education available to more people through these massive online courses, leading universities and industry professionals are democratizing access to education.

With its many options for lifelong learning and skill improvement, "The Rise of Online Learning Platforms: E-Learning and Beyond" demonstrates how online education has evolved into a vibrant and essential component of the educational landscape.

Chapter 7: Mastering the Information Age through Digital Literacy

- To succeed in today's information-driven society, readers of "Building Digital Literacy: Navigating the Information Age" will need to acquire the foundational abilities discussed in the book. The capacity to access, understand, and make appropriate use of digital resources (including but not limited to information, media, and technologies) is known as digital literacy.
- Important parts of this subject matter comprise:
- Acquiring Knowledge About Data Sources:
- One aspect of digital literacy is the capacity to identify trustworthy and questionable sources of information. In order to make educated decisions and stay away from false information, people need to know how to use the internet, how to assess websites, and how to identify credible sources.

Analyzing and Evaluating Online Content

- The development of critical thinking abilities is a key component of digital literacy since it equips people to assess information in a thoughtful and objective manner. Being able to make educated decisions in the digital realm requires challenging

assumptions, recognizing biases, and so on.
Media Competence:

- Acquiring media literacy is essential for digital fluency. Everyone needs to know the ins and outs of media bias, how to decipher visual and textual content in different digital formats, and how media messages are put together. Protection from Cyber Threats:

- Understanding and implementing online safety precautions is an essential component of digital literacy. Understanding the significance of secure online behaviors, being able to identify and avoid online risks, and protecting personal information are all part of this. Efficient Dialogue in Online Environments:

- Being able to communicate effectively in the digital space is part of digital literacy. This involves being aware of and following standard practices for appropriate online conduct, as well as being able to effectively communicate across a variety of digital mediums. Expertise in Technology:

- Having a basic understanding of technology is essential for digital literacy. From simple productivity apps to complex ones, people should feel at home with digital tools, software, and platforms.
Moral Issues to Think About:

- One aspect of digital literacy is being aware of the importance of digital ethics. Digital rights, privacy, and good digital citizenship are all part of this. Being respectful and ethically grounded is essential for individuals as they navigate digital spaces.

Flexibility and Ongoing Education:

- The lightning-fast development of new technologies is something that digital literacy recognizes. Keeping up with the latest technological developments and online trends requires an adaptable mindset and a dedication to lifelong learning.

Resolving Issues in Digital Settings:

- Being able to use various digital resources and tools to solve problems is what we mean when we talk about digital literacy. Anything from fixing technological problems to coming up with novel solutions by utilizing digital platforms is fair game.

Methods for Promoting Digital Literacy in the Classroom:

- Effective educational practices are necessary to build digital literacy. This includes creating training programs for teachers, encouraging a culture of lifelong learning in communities, and incorporating digital literacy into traditional school curricula.

"Building Digital Literacy: Navigating the Information Age" stresses the significance of preparing people to succeed in a society that is becoming more and more dependent on digital and information-driven systems. It gives people the tools they need to think critically, ethically, and confidently as they navigate the digital world.

Chapter 8: Utilizing Technology to Enhance Instruction

- "Building Digital Literacy: Navigating the Information Age" delves into the importance of being able to use digital tools and resources effectively in order to succeed in today's information-driven society. Learning how to effectively use information, assess information critically, and make a positive impact in the modern world are the primary goals of this theme.
- Important parts of this subject matter comprise:
- Being able to effectively use information:
- Putting an emphasis on finding, evaluating, and using information from a variety of sources. People who are digitally literate are better able to identify reliable sources, avoid being misled, and ultimately make better judgments. Media Competence:
- It focuses on the ability to interpret and comprehend messages conveyed through various forms of media, such as text, photos, and videos. The ability to critically analyze media content and identify possible biases or manipulations is a key component of digital literacy. Analytic Thinking:

- Individuals who are digitally literate are more likely to be able to think critically, which means they are more likely to challenge claims, weigh other viewpoints, and reach well-informed conclusions. Nowadays, when false information can spread like wildfire, this is more important than ever.

Knowledge about cybersecurity:

- Includes learning the fundamentals of cybersecurity, such as how to be safe when using the internet, how to keep personal information secure, and how to identify cyber threats. People who are literate in digital technologies are better able to safely traverse the online world.

Ability to Communicate Digitally:

- Includes fluency in the use of various digital mediums for the purpose of communication. Proper usage of social media, proper email protocol, and working together online are all part of this.

Knowledge of Technology:

- The ability to use and comprehend basic digital tools and technology is known as digital literacy. Among these skills is the ability to effectively use computers, software, and the internet for both work and play.

Flexibility and Ongoing Education:

- The capacity and desire to adapt to new technology are essential components of digital literacy, which is not a static concept. Those who are literate in digital technologies are more likely to pursue lifelong learning and keep up with the latest developments in the field. Implications of Technology Ethics:

- Discusses the moral issues raised by the application of technology. Behaving responsibly and respectfully in online interactions, recognizing the effects of technology on privacy, and respecting intellectual property rights are all aspects of digital literacy. Online Responsibilities:

- Embraces the idea that people should use technology ethically. Being a good online citizen means knowing and adhering to your rights and obligations, building supportive communities, and standing up against cyberbullying. Using Technology to Resolve Issues:

- Using one's problem-solving abilities in a contemporary digital setting. When people are digitally literate, they are better equipped to fix technological problems, learn new programs and platforms, and deal with digital obstacles. Recognizing the need for digital literacy in today's information-overloaded society, "Building Digital Literacy: Navigating the Information Age" explains how to acquire this skill. It teaches people how to be smart online, how to be safe when interacting with others, and how to make a difference in this digital world.

Chapter 9: Educational Cybersecurity: Protecting Online Instruction

- "Cybersecurity in Education: Safeguarding the Virtual Classroom" discusses the rising significance of securing online classrooms and other educational institutions against cybercriminals. Ensuring the security and privacy of sensitive information becomes crucial as education relies more and more on digital technologies and online platforms.
- Important parts of this subject matter comprise:
- Ensuring the security of data:
- Ensures that confidential information about students and employees is protected from intrusion, breaches, or other harmful actions. Protecting sensitive information, such as grades and personal details, requires stringent security measures to be put in place. Communication Security:
- Makes sure that all methods of communication used in the online classroom, including email, instant messaging, and video conferencing, are protected against spying and malware. The security of communication relies heavily on encryption and other forms of secure authentication.

Endpoint Protection:

- Think about how to keep computers, tablets, and smartphones safe when they're utilized in a virtual classroom. In order to protect the entire system from malware, ransomware, and other threats, it is important to implement endpoint security   measures.
Ensuring User Credibility and Permission:

- Protects the virtual classroom by implementing stringent user authentication procedures to restrict access to authorized users only. Safe login credentials, MFA, and role-based access control are   all   part   of   this.
Protecting Educational Software:

- Verifies that all program components utilized by the online school are secure and up-to-date with the latest security standards. To lessen the impact of security holes, these tools should be patched and   updated   regularly.
Reporting and Response to Incidents:

- Creates   procedures   for   handling   and documenting cyber events. Being prepared to handle security incidents such as breaches, illegal access, or any other problem in a timely and effective   manner   is   essential.
Educating and instructing:

- Informs   faculty,   students,   and   staff   on appropriate cybersecurity measures to take and possible dangers they may face. Individuals are better able to identify and react to possible security threats when a culture of awareness is fostered.

Protection of Networks:

- Pays special attention to protecting the VLE's underlying network architecture. Firewalls, intrusion detection systems, and other security measures should be put in place to prevent cyber assaults and illegal access. Adherence to Regulations:

- Guarantees adherence to applicable privacy and data protection laws. The rights and privacy of faculty and students are paramount, and schools must follow all applicable laws and regulations to do so. Ongoing Evaluation and Tracking:

- It involves doing frequent risk assessments and keeping an eye on the security posture of the virtual learning environment. Preventing security breaches is made easier by proactively finding and fixing vulnerabilities. "Cybersecurity in Education: Safeguarding the Virtual Classroom" recognizes that schools and other educational institutions are becoming more reliant on digital resources and highlights the importance of taking precautions to prevent cyberattacks. Educational stakeholders can provide a safe and effective virtual learning environment by implementing strong cybersecurity measures.

Chapter 10: Looking Ahead: How New Technologies Will Influence the Way We Teach in the Future

- As the title suggests, "Future Horizons: Emerging Technologies Shaping Tomorrow's Education" delves into the fascinating terrain of tech that is predicted to transform education in the years to come. Looking ahead to how new technologies may affect education in the future, this theme explores the revolutionary developments and game-changing possibilities of these tools.
- Important parts of this subject matter comprise:
- Computer programs that simulate human intelligence and how it learns:
- Examines the ways in which artificial intelligence and machine learning will impact the future of education through the provision of adaptive assessments, the personalization of learning experiences, and the assistance of educators in making data-driven decisions. Implementing Blockchain Technology in the Classroom:
- Explores the possibilities of blockchain technology to improve credentials, validate academic performance, and safeguard student records. The development of open, immutable educational systems can benefit from blockchain

technology.

The Worlds of Augmented and Virtual Reality:

- Plans for the widespread use of augmented and virtual reality (AR/VR) technology in classrooms to build more engaging and effective learning environments, such as virtual field excursions and interactive simulations.

Technologies for 5G networks:

- Delves into the effects of 5G technology on delivering more dependable and rapid internet access. With this, high-quality multimedia content integration, real-time collaboration, and streamlined online learning experiences are all within reach.

Web of Things (IoT) for the Classroom:

- Analyzes the potential of Internet of Things (IoT) devices to improve educational efficiency, keep tabs on classroom settings, and build interconnected learning ecosystems as a whole.

Reality Extension (XR):

- Imagine a future when virtual reality (VR), augmented reality (AR), and mixed reality (MR) merge into extended reality (XR), allowing for more engaging and immersive learning experiences that blend the real and virtual worlds.

Automation and robotics:

- Investigates the potential of robotics and automation in the classroom, from actual robots to handling administrative duties so teachers may

devote more time to individual students.
Biometric Systems:

* Investigates the possibility of biometric technology for secure authentication, monitoring attendance, and creating individualized learning plans according to a student's physiological or behavioral traits.
Platforms for Adaptive Learning:

* Imagine a future where adaptive learning systems use data analytics and artificial intelligence to monitor and adjust course materials in real time based on each student's unique requirements, paving the way for more efficient and successful educational paths.
Empowering Students with Quantum Computing:

* Delves into the ways quantum computing could revolutionize the solution of intricate mathematical and cryptographic issues, opening up exciting new avenues for cutting-edge research and computational assignments in the classroom.

To reimagine education in the future, "Future Horizons: Emerging Technologies Shaping Tomorrow's Education" encourages readers to see a world where these innovative tools complement one another. In this theme, we take a look at how these new technologies could change education in the future by analyzing their possible uses and consequences.